Mental Masturbation
Quit Playing with Yourself

Poetry & Prose

by

Dessie Bey

First printing (-C-)

ISBN: 978-0-557-45731

db Point of View Publishing

Contact: dbeypoet@yahoo.com

Phone: 412-464-0321

READ *at your own risk*

Observation of a Crack Addict

I saw the greatest of the best of
minds in this century of my time
shattered piece by piece.

Desire's illusion dragging men
and women to the lowest pit of
hell on earth, chasing the ever
eluding dragon. Puff, puff, and
puffing and going up in smoke.

Souls becoming vacant temples
inhabited by bloodsucking
roaches crawling over the scum of
their minds sacred earth for a
piece... just a little piece of the
rock.

While a still sane and wise elder
is rocking... rocking the soul of
the infidels in the bosom of
Abraham. As they burn in
perdition here on Earth. Rock of
ages, cleft for me.

Gazing at what seems to be the Rock of Gibraltar. Fools Gold on the bowl of your glass blown pipe that you handle as if “fragile” was stamped on it. You tenderly caress that pipe even more than me in our best love making. I can’t compete.

And you suck on the lip of that pipe like you never sucked my neck. You watch the feel-good, you

watch the feel-good travel through the stem, you tremble as before ejaculation. Your eyes close as you sink into tranquility, as if we reached that great abyss together.

I allowed her to be your girl for a season. But this bitch has ingenuously stolen the very heart of you. How could I let you get away?

She rocks your world as an erupting volcano. Shaking you to the core violently yet pleasurably, but counterfeit.

The crack, white molten, hot rock shrinking... Shrinking into every swelling cell of your tabernacle. The chlorine, ammonia aroma fills the room with the deceit of pure pollution.

White smoke encircles serpentinely around your head. You're still sucking, not even realizing that only traces of carbon are left in the bowl. It matters no more to you that it's not sparkling clear and that the build up of residual fornication is choking your soul to the core.

You don't even realize that your flesh has unerringly regressed back to dust and ash. Your reflection is ghostly.

II

Embracing the bowl of your treasured pipe ever so tenderly... more tenderly than every my ass... your fingertips are melted to the bone, glued to the glass and you are numb to that fact. Climaxing... trying to hold on to the promise. The glass cracks as your god descends and all who love you along with her.

That quick escape holds you captive. You're left gasping for the breath of life.
Breathe...breathe, damn it, breathe!

They left you hanging... they left you hanging for dead. Even I knew it was too unbelievably incredible. Even I knew it was too good to be true.

They left you. Hanging here.
Hooked on a mythical paradise.
Breathe, damn it, breathe!

Time out... Another one bites the
dust... All roaches scatter.

And we mourn in the alley, and
we mourn on the next abandoned
temple, and we mourn on our
grand mama's grave. And we
promise this rendezvous on
satan's fantasy island is over.

A mere encounter of foreplay is
all I need. It's all I need... It's all I
need.

Bread of heaven... God – I need –
Feed me... God I need – Till I
want...

Shame covers your eyes. Then
you notice the rawness of your
fingertips

...Till I want, till I want... no more, no more, no more.

Back from the frolic for the moment. Walking, walking, trotting, jogging, running. Searching, searching for a trace of your unblemished spirit.

God, don't look in the glass, you might see yourself. All that's left is the shadow. Look, look into your heart before you cross the threshold, before you plan your next suffocating suicide mission. Get a grip.

What day is it? Is it the same day as yesterday? Is it tomorrow?

Time out... Time out of mind... I'm singing the blues, it must be... Yes it's got to be Sunday.

No... it's still today... Some time today.

You're lost in a time warp. The very soul of you vanished while you were drowning in your own deception. While swimming in your own vomit. You attempted to back stroke and to look up, but denial sucked your breath with every hit. Breathe, damn it, breathe!

Rock of ages cleft for me. In the bosom of Abraham rock my soul, comfort me. Save me from myself... from Puff... this mighty beast... the magic dragon.

Stop the chase! You can never capture the feel-good again. It's never as good as the first time. Stop the chase! It's no longer perfection and grace. It's no longer a smile on my face.

She used to be glorious and grand. I'd romance her only when I desired her. Oh, I was on top of the world but, it was oh so temporary. She became the bottomless pit and I'm floating in her spit.

Finesse and confidence crashed. The crack had sucked up the charm. Style, poise, and charisma are virtues of the past. The bottom has dropped and here I crawl.

Me, the cool cat is now a rabid dawg. I can't hide. Crack won't let me be... won't let me be discreet. My name is running up and down the street. She keeps calling my name. Constantly nagging... I can't shake her, I can't shake her...

I'm running rampant. Like an uncaged animal... The dawgs are in the street. The dawgs are in the heartless, forsaken streets. Dis-eased by the euphoric feel-good. Comatosed, no mental capacity. I feel no more.

Are you feeling me?

III

Time out… you want to go to rehab. Rehab! You're not on meth! Crack-head! Go to jail! Go directly to jail! You do not pass go in the hood! You go directly to jail!

Help me now! The small voice inside screams.

Cop a plea. Present your case with a sob-sad look… We're going to work this out baby. Just one more chance. We're going to work this… we're going to work this thing out.

Your mouth is moving, but you have no voice – you ain't saying nothing. You really think you're saying something. Who is that conversation with… the invisible? The mythical? The feel-good?

Oh so cunning. Our life has been a masquerade.

Our baby was born screaming. Remember Crack Baby "Exhibit A"... See your baby on TV. Our moment of fame. Our baby was writhing wirily in pain for the world to see. See... See my baby, Crack Baby "Exhibit A", held like an animal... foaming at the mouth. Feenin... hungry like a wolf. Howling, squealing. Now our baby is in the street. Killing, killing, killing! Never had a chance... see our baby, now our baby is in the streets.

Who unlocked the gates of hell to let the angel of living death out? What power in this world conjured up this spirit of damnation on earth and planted it in the house of creation? Who indeed let the dawgs out? Who indeed released this diabolical evil?

Oh so cunning.

Well-come home. Everything of value is hidden in places that even I probably won't remember. Even that is better than it being pan handled in the street.

I can't phantom your lips on mine. Knowing that the crack takes you to animalistic states of inhumane pleasures and still always leaves you wanting.

But oh my dear, I open again. Knowing I can do better. You can do better.

IV

It really was the best of times. It really was the worst of times. It seemed to be.

Who knew?

You were climbing the ladder of success to reach rock bottom. It wasn't how high you could go, but precisely how low. You were silk and satin but you turned into tattered lace.

Who knew? The feel-good was good when it was good. Coolness was your name in every state of the game. You were up, in, on and there was no shame. No shame, not even when elders and dignitaries crossed your path.

You begged them for a dollar; you begged them for a dime. Get yourself clean, get yourself up...

Look at yourself, you ran out of time.

I looked at my tattered lace persona that used to be silk, that used to be satin. I held my head high but I was down so damn low I had to look up at my feet. I cried for my mama. I had become the one that only a mother could love... MAMA! I have to catch up with my Mama before she gets away. She loves me more than anything... I got to catch up with my God fearing Mama.

Mama, remember back in the day when you loved all my pain away. I'm paining now Mama. Won't you help me please? I'm paining now Mama, I need the feel-good Mama! Mama, Mama, Mama! Look at your son... Mama, Mama, Mama! Look at your daughter... Mama, Mama I'm down on my knees!

How did birth of a blessing become a beast? What matter of blaspheme are you? In the public eye, no shame. From consideration and compassion, peace and love you came and this crack in you released demons creating havoc that no man can tame.

Get off your knees son. Get off your knees daughter. Your tears are just a stream of lies. I'm walking away today. I haven't known you since you violated my house. Get yourself clean. Ain't there no sun in your mind? Since that crack explosion, you've become a bastard and a motherless child.

Mama, Mama! I need the feel-good. I ain't feeling right. Mama you going to make me... You going to make me rob and hurt somebody... so I can get it on tonight.

Mama, Mama, Mama! Don't walk away! My stomach is turning! Damn it to hell! Let me dust myself off and go out and play. Somebody's going to have to pay. I'm inside out. The feel-good has flipped. I need some food... Puke—aahg—puke—aahg... Flat on my face... In the mist of regurgitation... I'm feenin' feel-good, feel-good, feel-good... Gawd, where am I? God – Dog... Dawg – Gawd...

Quit kicking me, I ain't your Dawg... gawd... God... I got to kick it! Why's it so dark here. Quit stepping over me. My Gawd is turning on me... Aahg—puke, puke—aahg... I need the feel-good. I'm hungry. Give me a taste?

Dawg back to the vomit... Oh God, —aahg, puke. I got to find a way out of here. Where am I?

Why's there no light in their eye? Why's there no light in my eye?

Where's the door? Time? Time? There use to be a natural order of time... Daylight coming, daylight coming and I want to go home.

Mama— Where's the gate? Get off of me! How do I get this monkey off my back? Don't touch me! How do I get out of this wicked, God forsaken place?

Mama— Get up off your knees and look to the hills... Mama— I can't find the gate! Where's the door? Whose are these? Who is that? Who am I?

Come on... you're no stranger here... Go ahead!

Taste and see, I hate to see you suffer... You ain't going nowhere. Where's your dream. Here's your pipe. But while you down there on your knees... A favor for a favor. Here I am, here I am...

The feel-good... Yea, the feel-good... What you won't do for... for the feel-good.

No! No! I am free... I am free...

Well-come home.

I'm going to walk with this peace... Out of this paradigm. I'm leaving this scene. I'm going to walk out of my pipe dream nightmare. Yes I am, Yes I am.

I can see... I can see clearly now...

See the beautiful unicorn in the distance!

Well-come home.

Dark Hole

I'm crawling
Into a dark hole

I'm searching
For the light of my soul

Skeletons
From the closet
Haunt the secret corridors
Of my mind

The crawl space
Is much to narrow
For the light to penetrate
Through and through

So I repent
Of all un-Godly thoughts
And all idle events

This place
Of no retreat
This point
Of no return
Can cause a desolate heart
To burn

So I yearn
And I search
For the light of my soul

To guide my mind
Out of this world's
Dark hole

Fear

In the face of Goliath
I step up to my demon

I look in the mirror of my shadow
And search for the light in back of my third eye

Exploring the residue of hurt
Pain and abuse
I'm attacked by thoughts of despair
From attempting to unlock fear

Unlatching the grasp
The cesspool burst forth full blast
The stench of life's possible impossibilities
Irritates my membranes
With reality's – broken illusions
I spit Goliath into the great abyss

Taking back my courage
And destroying fear's myth

I accept the challenge
Of living without dictation and outside strife
Just being myself
And loving my life

In the mirror
The demon being slain
Momentary
I'm out of my mind in the invisible
And
My soul is worth the gain

And I say
"Devil, don't even try to remember my name"
As the shadow reflected to cast the light

I close the third eye for now

And continue to live a “normal”
life

Preach

Let your heart break
That your cry can be heard
From invisible
To the
Invisible
To the manifestation

Beware
My dear
Beware
Thought manifest
Both evil and good

Beware
My dear
Beware

Be careful of the quest
Having nothing to say

But “Glory to God in the highest
And on earth peace, goodwill
toward men”

Surely your heart won’t break
If you allow your mind to bend

Mind being conscious

And
Soul being ‘sub...’
Subconscious
The saving grace of conscious
Thought’s perversion

Consciously
Stretch out to the brink

Faith won’t let you sink

Be baptized in the unconscious
To be revived

From the conscious mind's stink

When the mind
Conscious and 'sub...'
Become one and agree
Glory Hallelujah
We'll rock the powers that be
Glory Hallelujah
Thank God
Thank God for being set free

And it can be done
In the physical
In this earth
You can be
In harmony with God
When you allow your mind
A new birth
Yes
You can be perfect
Perfection being your best
Pay no mind to what folks say

Whether you passed or failed their test

Everlasting life
Is living forever
Mentally
If you can't believe nothing else

Can I take you there?
Are you ready to go?

For those of you who have an ear
Hear what the Spirit sayeth to churches

Let go and let God
Let your Sub-conscious flow

The Life A Spiritual Journey

Somebody told me
I was living the life
Having it "all" meant absolutely nothing to me

"All" was an illusion of what I could not see
Looking through rose-colored glasses
I took the world by storm
"Eat, drink, and be merry"
Was the dreadful norm

Doing a 9 to 5
Five days a week
Every day was 'party-time'
Mind altering substances did reek
Smoke-filled weekends – all mine

Life in the fast lane

Wheelin' and dealin' with much game

Living to the extreme
The ultimate "I" reigned supreme
Nothing really mattered but the blow and the Joe

Living hi – on the hog
But paying the cost
Subconsciously
Because my soul was lost

On the surface who could ask for more
Mind below sea-level
Drowning in manure

Suffocating in the glittery pleasures of life

"I", "me", "mine"
Was a spiritual detour

At 11 on Sunday I was praising the Lord

Ignoring the stench of being tainted from the night before

My soul wants to steal away

And stay in the fold

But my mind says

"Too late –

You've already been bought and sold"

You belong to

"Me", "myself" and "I"

No way God can get in

So don't even try

Keep on getting down

In the muck and the mire

Your home will be an everlasting fire

Not after while

Bye and bye
On earth hell will face you eye to eye

Stop you in your tracks

Just when you think you got over
Then you realize for the first time
That you are actually sober!!!
Caught in a whirlwind
Suddenly the blues kick in

As living reveals her sin

Damn
You've been pimped by the good life

Visions blurred
And mind full of strife

Looking through rose-colored
glasses

It's the beginning of the end
Of your life

Gone Crazy

The trains
I hear them
All in my brain

Ma said
When you hear trains
In your brains
You soon be gone

Mind be gone
Somewhere in the sound
The sound of that train

Travelin' somewhere
Beyond time and space
Know not where

Mind be lost
In the sound of that train
The train

I hear them
All in my brain

Between my ears
Inside my head

A strange engineer is laying track
To take me back
To somewhere

In the dark
Where I see the invisible
And here the train
In the dark
Where I touch the untouchable
And here the train
In the dark
Real is a dream
And a dream is a lie
You can be the floor of the earth
Or transform beyond the sky

The trains
I hear them
All in my brain

Ma said
When you hear those trains
In your brains
You soon be gone

You soon be gone

Bye-Bye

Gangsta

Live by the sword
Die by the sword

You take one more innocent
One more hope
The wrath of God be upon you
And not even the prison ministry
Will be able to redeem
Your God forsaken soul

A human who takes
The life of an innocent
Is null and void
Is not worthy
Of the blood in his veins

Reap what you sow
In God speed

Media Blitz

I don't need the media
Telling me that 8 out of 10 murders
Remain Black on Black crime
That is nothing new
Trying to sanitize the self hatred to homicide

The rage has escalated
To a heartless, unconscious evil
An evil that escapes love
Mama and Daddy even devoid of the capability of **love**
Mama's nails, hair, and sexual infirmities take **priority**
And baby's just a by-product of "the look"
And daddy... yea... well...
Still mama's baby, daddy's maybe
But still all baby boy or baby girl knows is what he and she sees

And the darkest hour is 24 – 7
There's a hope that's an illusion
There is no light at the end of the never ending tunnel
And the vision is a distorted black light
Where is the love

An honor student in Chi-Town is literally stomped to death

Where is the love
A 5 year old is used as a shield
For a punk so-called gangster-- who won't own his bullet
Where is the love
I have a plenty

But how, how, how
Do I touch your soul
Your eyes emit death
Where is the love
I'm looking for life in you

Life in you
I'm looking for it

You're... walking
You're... talking
I'm looking for life in you

How, how, how...
Do I kill a zombie
So life will prevail

I'm mercilessly angry
Down right mad

Because of you
I can't raise a clenched fist for power
Because of you
I can't raise my "V" fingers for peace
Because of you...
I've stooped to a new lowness

Because I want you to feel...

I want you to feel
The pain you inflict

Now that's news worthy

Life

The illusion is
That
You really ain't
What
You think you are
And
That
You really ain't
Who
You think you are
And
That
You really don't
Have what you think you have
And
Life ain't
No bag of weed
And life
Ain't even
A bag of salt and vinegar chips

Crack Baby

Your soul has no savior touched
And your living lifelessness prevails
Kill it before it grows
--Exhibit A--
From the pit of hell
Born to destroy life
--Exhibit B--
You must go back
From whence you came

You must go back
From whence you came

So God-fearing living
Can stand a ghost of a chance

Crack Baby to Criminal

Born into this world
In pain of withdrawal
Dry heaves, the shakes and hallucination
How frightening
Your first sensations

On exhibit
They held you up in front of a TV camera
As if an animal
As if in a freak show

You didn't know
You're a new born baby
Screaming in pain
Wrenching and cringing
Yearning for a hit
Not even a day old
And in rehab

Love never penetrated
Meth was your only stimulation
Your attention span is too short
You have the strength of a bull
And no consciousness
No heart in your mind

Shiny trinkets caught your eye
And fast moving wheels spinning
So when you saw the sparkling cross
Hanging from the perpetrators neck
When you saw the spinning rims
On the perpetrators car
You wanted to be just like him

And so you got a gun
By hook or crook
You were going to get you one
And at the tender age of 10
Baby boy is on the run

Crack High

Violently you cough
You choke
Your body's rejection is part of the high
Your skin pits and splits
Teeth decay
You're being eaten alive
And this is feel good to you

I Never Thought I'd See the Day

I never thought I'd see the day
When a mother would sell her child
And walk away

I never thought that I would see the day
When a child would kill
For an exhilarating thrill

I never wanted to see the day

Mother against daughter
Father against son
Revelations
Prophecy
This world undone

Believed it
But I never wanted to see the day

That man would describe themselves as d-o-g
Opposite G-o-d

I never wanted to see the day
Back in the day
It was written
So it is

But I never wanted to see the day
That the way of the world is to self destruct
Our sons, brothers and fathers
Keep killing each other

And our daughters, sisters and mothers
Sell there souls for a piece of the rock
And become the female counterpart, b-i-t-c-h
To the d-o-g
And itch

For a moment of counterfeit foreplay

I never wanted to see the day

I never wanted to see the day
When “of the people, by the people, for the people”
Sang a peace song
And war was declared across the land

I never wanted to see the day
When the anti-Christ antics
Would be an international game to play
I never wanted to see the day
This is the day
That the Lord has made
We should rejoice and be glad

Babylon is fallen
Babylon is fallen

The ram emulates the lamb
Baring fangs
The great whore snarls
For fear of global retaliation / revelations
To gain power over all

I never wanted to see the day
This is the day
Shall we rejoice?

And after all
d-a-w-g still equals dog
And really ain't best friend to man
A bitch will never do
But a woman sure can

Damn...
I never wanted to see the day

Summertime: The Criminalization of a Nation

For Ja-esha Scott, 5 year old African American girl handcuffed by St. Petersburg FL police at Fairmont Park Elementary School – March 2005

We wanted you to rise
We thought we had arrived
But here it is 2005
And we still striving
Striving, striving to survive
They cuffed our little baby girl
And she was only 5

Hush little baby
Hush little baby
Don't you cry
Mommy and daddy
Mommy and daddy
Somewhere
Somewhere, Somewhere
Standing by

Headlines for a day
The atrocity white-washed away
Black Males fearing nothing
Is anybody else feeling this decay

Inhumane homicide, genocide
Self inflicted living suicide
My heart bleeds
Fathers and Sons and Brothers
Being railroaded
Cause they won't legalize weed
The billion dollar business plan
For the black man to succeed

But dare they let us
Meet our peoples need
To allow the Black Man to actually
Be "The Man" indeed

In this parasitic society
They locking prison cells

And throwing away the key
Criminalizing our men-children
Based on reading skills
At the elementary level of grade 3

Is anybody hearing me
This ain't meant to be

Gestapo police
Authorized to commit murder in the first degree
"Bulls eye", shoot to kill
And they did
12 year old Michael Ellerbee

Undercover evil
Masquerading in Christ-like fashion
Exposed for even the blind to see
Yet here we sit content
Shaking our heads and doing nothing

Can’t you hear the echo
Echo, echo, echo
From the past
Freedom ain't free
Free, free, free
Time to break the slave mentality

One of these, one of these
One of these mornings
You gonna rise up
To save a nations stolen legacy
And grab our innate purity
That was criminalized in a lost mind

Suffocated in the stagnant humidity
Of an overcast…
Fogged up…
Lazy…
Hazy…
Goddamned…. Summertime

Peace

The doves are falling
The hawks are calling
As the raven devours
The soul of creation

The gulls are grabbing
Everything in sight
Proclaiming
They know best
What's in the heart of a raven

The caucus walks
Homeless, jobless
Mindless
Mindful of the day when
He nested in the shelter
Of freedom
Before the eagle
Spanned his wing
Doves were free to fly

By Fire This Time

And so it is
The apocalypse

The day of evil
Stand in a holy place

And so be it
The sea is contaminated - boiling
- on fire
The fowl and fish toxic
The ozone, purposely depleted
The vegetation is brittle

And there is no love

The earth has turned
On the earthlings

Exhausted from abuse
On the verge of self-implosion

As in the day of Noah
Not by water
But fire this time
And so it is
The apocalypse

The day of evil
Stand in a holy place
And so be it
Mother against daughter
Father against son
Growing in destruction
Fire and heavy artillery
Visions of arming themselves with guns

Babies making babies
How do you love
Generations dead at the root
The heart waxed cold
As in the day of Noah
Not by water

But fire this time

And so it is
The apocalypse

The day of evil
Stand in a holy place

And so be it
The sun refuses to shine
There's a draught in heart of man
Nations fall – Nations rise
The Red Horse
The White Horse
The Black Horse
None forever stand

The sky bleeds the blood
Who shall be able to stand
Is there no balm
No forgiveness in the land

The sky bleeds the blood
The day of reckoning is at hand

And so it is
The apocalypse
The day of evil
Stand in a holy place

And so be it…

And the Hand Still Writes

And he delivered the Afrikans
Into the Amerikkkans
And the Amerikkkans
Forced them
In inhumane ways
As chattel
To serve
In lewdness
Enslaved to self
Greed encompasses the heart
Lord – please – have mercy

Treated less than human
These Afrikans
SURVIVED
And were delivered

These Afrikans survived
And were freedom bound
And fought for their rights

Civil rights
Human rights remain illusive
In the hearts of men
And these Afrikans flourished
At a point in time
And needed to become

So they overcame
And integrated
And greed encompassed their heart
Lord – please – have mercy

Struggling to become
These Afrikan Amerikkkans
SURVIVED
And were delivered

These Afrikans survived
And desired to be
Other than who they were
So they attempted to assimilate

Into an unfamiliar Amerikkkan
Culture and forget

Forget the pain of slavery
Forget the evils suffered
Forget their kindred spirits
And become individuals
And separate themselves from self
And desired to capitalize
Instead of fair trade
And greed encompassed their heart
Lord – please – have mercy

Estranged from themselves
These motherless children
SURVIVED

And were delivered
These motherless children
Divorced from self and history

Traded their soul
For an illusion of life
Sending their mind
In helter-skelter mode

Not coming or going
Moving fast going nowhere
Ever wanting, never satisfied
Searching for comfort in an eyeful

As your Spirit yearns for third eye substance
That escapes your mental capacity
Your lost soul wrestles
For a space in your conscious mind

A possible breakthrough in a dream
In a nightmare your souls grasps
At fragments of your archetype
But ego demands attention

Lord – please – have mercy

On a comatose subconscious
zombie people

SURVIVING

To be

Again

Delivered

Amalgamation

We once walked the planet
Dark skinned and nappy headed

We once walked the planet
I mean – skin as dark as night
And hair curled clam tight

We once walked the planet
Until, until seeds from forbidden fruit
Once strange fruit
Rooted

We once walked the planet
I mean – inner courts
Kings and Queens
Inner of inner courts
Then intercourse
Opposing attractions

Off-course
Confluence

We once walked the planet
Never accepting one another

Too Black
Not Black enough
You lack

So light
So bright
Just right

And so
We are
No more

We once walked the planet
Every one of us a shade of
different hue

We once walked the planet
Now enter in the age of
transparency

Where have all the flowers gone?

A Lily in the Valley A Spiritual Journey

From above or from below

On the spiritual realm

You have no choice

Go with the flow

Dipping and dabbing in the darkness of night

My light so dim

I didn't recognize him

Nagging and pulling on my 6th and 7th sense

Only retreating when I fell off of the fence

Life flashing before me like an open book

To God be praises for allowing me a 2nd look

The world playing me

Like a favorite 45 record
Over and over temptation soared
Until my mind disjoined from that invisible cord

Being sucked in the vacuum of hell
The battled pursued
Thank God, my soul was well

I saw through my 3rd eye
And I had an ear to hear
As my temple was the ground
For good and evil to appear

Emotions familiar from the past
Beckoning me to succumb to evil at last

My Spirit being extracted
Through a tunnel of darkness
Thank God for Jesus

The light that he cast

There was struggling and fear
Which seem to go on an eternity of time
Thank God for the victory in Jesus
Our Soul to Spirit life line

The company we keep
Accounts for the situations we reap

Good and evil cannot occupy the same space
If you are not evenly yoked
There is a battle
And life is a competitive race

Mentally on the run
Never to rest
Spirit and Soul at odds
Mind seems in control

But totally undone

2 forces of opposite nature
Driving or drawing at the speed of light
One represents forever day
The other eternal night

Aluminous radiance
Breaking from the bowels of the earth
My spirit escapes
My soul gives way
I lay in the peace of the glow
With fiery swords at the gate
The sound of quick rushes
Rushing for my Spirit's sake
Thank God for transplantation
In the Garden, my Soul's estate

The safety zone
Where the demons of life

Will have no home

In the brilliance, the quietness, the stillness
The purest of light
Feeling the bliss of peace
Blinded, only seeing through God's sight

Not a player
Just an observer of the truth
Satan's forces could not prevail
And Jesus' unconditional love is the proof
No tales of fear
No tears to shed
Just know, when you least expect it
God is right there

Using all available to bring you down
Demons attack you

With worldly pleasures
That makes the world go round

Creeping into the privacy of your thoughts
Shadows of negative vibes
Pacing, trying to have their lot
Infiltrating the peace that dwells within
Coming at me by trying to destroy my next to kin

Dragging my seed through the grapes of wrath
But what God has created
Satan can't have

Thank God for what he has allowed for me
Most of all I thank God for his grace and mercy
Claims I made for what was mine

Turned into hell over a matter of time

Striving to make it daily by society's book
The ways and means of work
Led to hook or crook
From the street to the bible
Which ever worked first
Would make my life secure and viable

The mixture could literally drive you insane
"By any means necessary" in Jesus name

Partying morning, noon and night
Miscues the nature of God's delight

"Eat, drink, and be merry" was the way

Day was night and night was day
Creating a dragon
That only God could slay
Deep in the darkness
In the thickness of gloom

Demons await
Taking form, they loom
Physically they surround
Hooded robes
Candles in hand
Chanting, a ceremony, and you are their lamb

The demons will follow night in, night out
Plaguing your mind with invisible sights
Having you see wrong
What you know is right

You're left helpless

Only God can win this fight
He beams his light aimed straight to the soul
Injecting his power that no demon can hold

A glimmer of hope
Breaks through the night
Faith burst forward
First day light

Promises from heaven
Kept by the faith
No more darkness and strife
With God first in your life

The love of God is no secret to men
With satan's crafty discretion's
Demons can camouflage Jesus
Your best friend
"To thine own self be true"

A quote worthy of thought
If followed
Your soul will never be on the auction block

"Lo I am with you even to the end"
That is word
And believe, with all you go through
God will descend
To ascend

Take you to another level
A new plain, dimension
If you're willing to go
In the Spirit of God
Let it flow

Choosing Jesus' way
Love, peace, long suffering, mercy and grace

A few of his attributes to help you win this race

The unseen can be friend or foe
Whatever your choice
It's a positive or negative flow

Your soul is the pure connection
Search for God's own heart
Within you
You will find
The power of eternal resurrection

That I Am

I am
That I am

The balance

That gives you compassion

I am
That I am

The balance
The heart of the mind

I am
That I am

God be with us

www.ingramcontent.com/pod-product-compliance
Ingram Content Group UK Ltd.
Pitfield, Milton Keynes, MK11 3LW, UK
UKHW020219250726
13967UKWH00001B/83

9 780557 457311